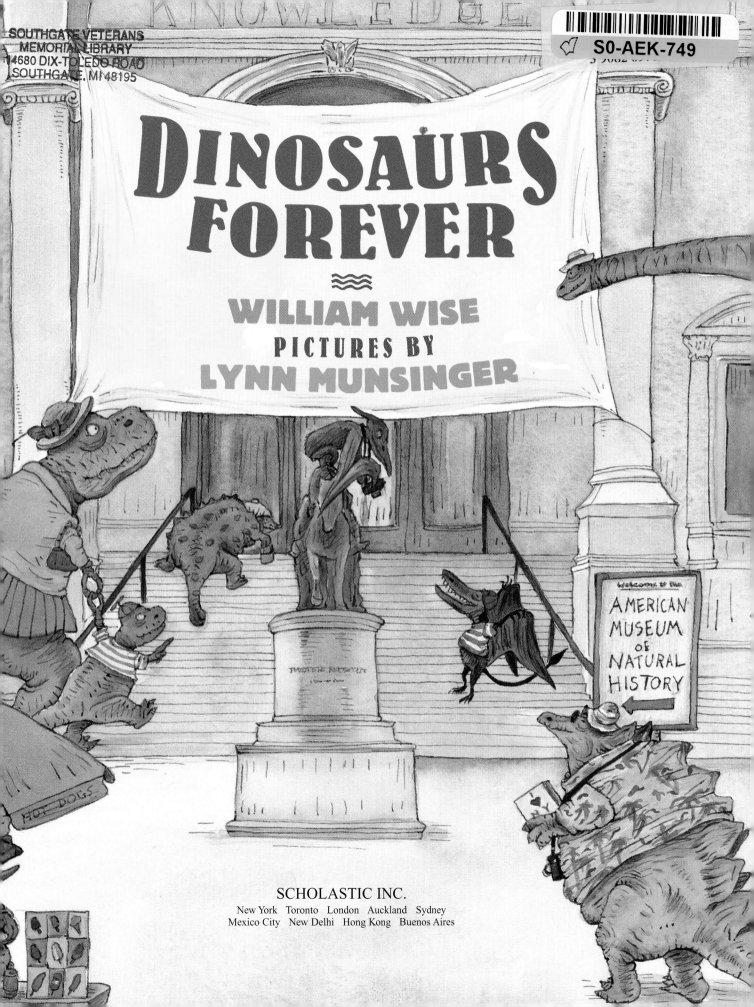

DINOSAURS FOREVER

WILLIAM WISE
PICTURES BY
LYNN MUNSINGER

SCHOLASTIC INC.

New York Toronto London Auckland Sydney
Mexico City New Delhi Hong Kong Buenos Aires

For Brian —L. M.

Special thanks to paleontologist J. Lynett Gillette for
reviewing the manuscript and illustrations.

ISBN 0-439-31780-0

Text copyright © 2000 by William Wise.
Illustrations copyright © 2000 by Lynn Munsinger.
All rights reserved.
Published by Scholastic Inc., 555 Broadway, New York, NY 10012,
by arrangement with Dial Books for Young Readers, a division of Penguin Putnam Inc.
SCHOLASTIC and associated logos are trademarks and/or
registered trademarks of Scholastic Inc.

12 11 10 9 8 7 6 5 4 3 2 1   3 4 5 6/0

Printed in the U.S.A.   14

First Scholastic printing, October 2001

The full-color artwork was prepared using pen-and-ink and watercolor.
It was then scanner-separated and reproduced as red, blue, yellow, and black halftones.
Designed by Julie Rauer and Nancy R. Leo-Kelly

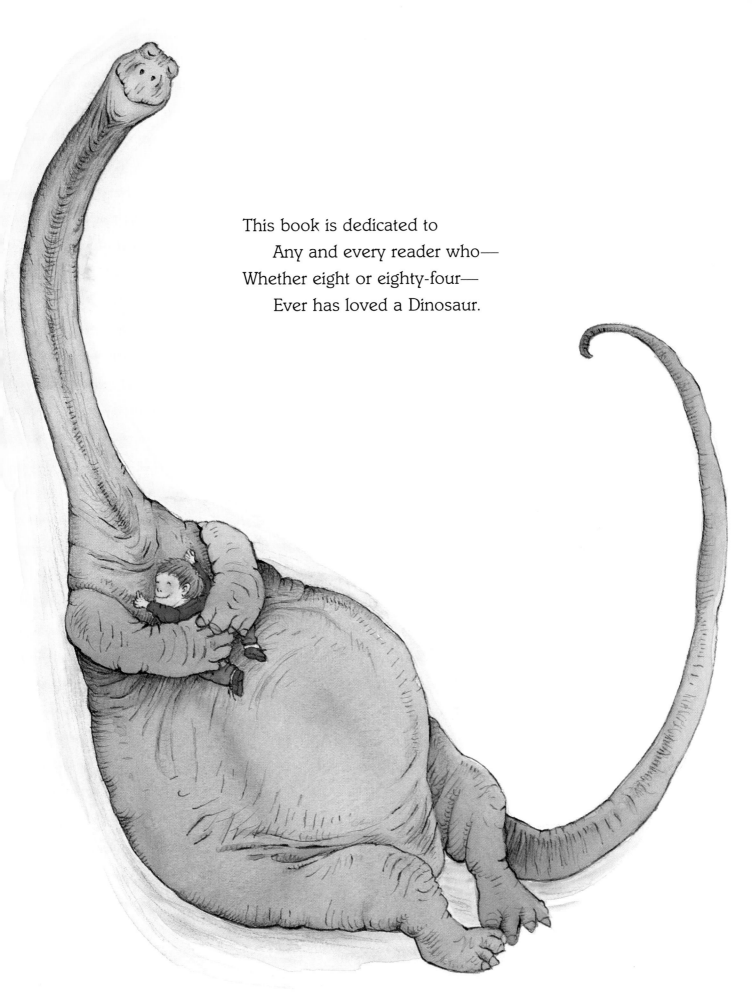

This book is dedicated to
    Any and every reader who—
Whether eight or eighty-four—
    Ever has loved a Dinosaur.

Pronunciation Guide

Triassic	(try-AS-ick)
Jurassic	(juh-RAS-ick)
Cretaceous	(kre-TAY-shus)
Camptosaurus	(kamp-tuh-SAW-rus)
Velociraptor	(ve-los-uh-RAP-tor)
Triceratops	(try-SER-uh-tops)
Tyrannosaurus Rex	(ty-ran-oh-SAW-rus rex)
Apatosaurus	(a-pat-uh-SAW-rus)
Ornitholestes	(or-nith-o-LESS-teez)
Gorgosaurus	(gor-guh-SAW-rus)
Deinonychus	(dy-no-NY-kus)
Allosaurus	(al-uh-SAW-rus)
Ankylosaurus	(an-kil-o-SAW-rus)
Pterodactyls	(ter-uh-DAK-tills)
Rhamphorhynchus	(ram-fo-RINK-us)
Dimorphodon	(dy-MORE-fuh-don)
Pteranodon	(ter-AN-uh-don)
Maiasaura	(my-a-SAW-ra)
Stegosaurus	(steg-uh-SAW-rus)
Ichthyosaurs	(ICK-thee-uh-sawrs)
Plesiosaurs	(PLEE-zee-uh-sawrs)
Mosasaurs	(MOZE-uh-sawrs)

MILLIONS AND MILLIONS OF YEARS AGO

Millions and millions of years ago
The world was warm,
As I'm sure you know.
There never was ice,
And there never was snow,
Millions and millions of years ago.

There were no houses,
There were no men,
There were no women or children then.
There were no dogs,
There were no cats,
No hogs or frogs,
No rats or bats.
But oh, there were monsters,
As I'm sure you know,
Millions and millions of years ago.

And so I think,
For an hour or two,
We'll go back in time,
Which is fun to do,
And visit the world,
When the world was new,
To meet the fabulous reptiles there,
The beasts of Earth, and Sea, and Air,
To watch that incredible Monster Show,
Of millions and millions of years ago.

THREE DINOSAUR AGES

The Dinosaurs lived
During three different Ages,
When the whole world was empty and spacious.
And each Age long ago
Had a name you should know—
Triassic—Jurassic—Cretaceous!

Yes, the Dinosaurs lived
During three different Ages,
Their lifestyle rude and ungracious.
They slept, and they ate,
And gained far too much weight,
In Triassic—Jurassic—Cretaceous!

Now, some Dinosaurs quarreled,
And some Dinosaurs fought,
For a number were fierce and pugnacious,
Though they lived with their peers,
For millions of years,
In Triassic—Jurassic—Cretaceous!

DINOSAUR COLORS

What colors were the Dinosaurs?
  The fact is, no one knows.
We're only sure that each had skin
  That stretched from head to toes.

It might be, Camptosaurus
  Was a leafy shade of green,
So when he strolled among the reeds,
  He scarcely could be seen.

Perhaps Velociraptor
  Was bright orange in his youth,
Though your guess is as good as mine,
  And no one knows the truth.

I've heard it said Triceratops
    Was colored navy blue.
No doubt a splendid sight to see,
    Provided it was true.

But one thing I am certain of—
    I truly cannot think
That huge Tyrannosaurus Rex
    Could ever have been pink!

DINOSAUR DINNERS

Oh, Dinosaurs, Dinosaurs,
    What do you eat?
"Sir, *I* dine on green leaves,
    And *he* dines on red meat!

"I eat the green leaves,
    And never eat others,
But he eats his friends,
    And even his brothers.

"Yes, I dine on green leaves,
    Which makes *me* vegetarian,
And he dines on red meat,
    Which makes *him* a barbarian."

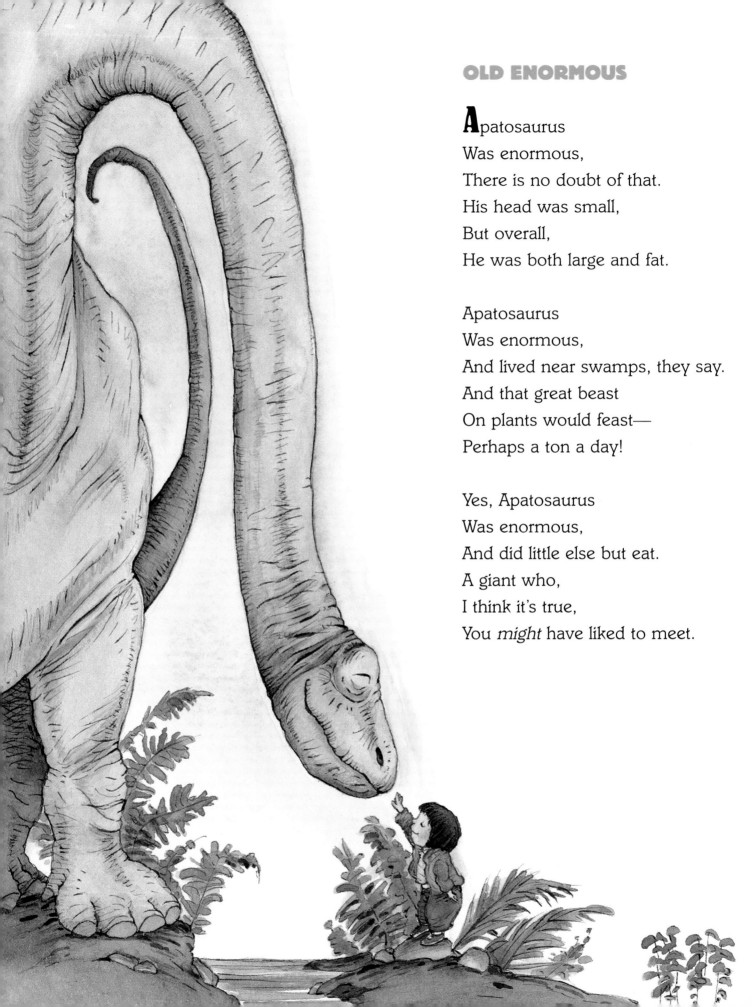

OLD ENORMOUS

Apatosaurus
Was enormous,
There is no doubt of that.
His head was small,
But overall,
He was both large and fat.

Apatosaurus
Was enormous,
And lived near swamps, they say.
And that great beast
On plants would feast—
Perhaps a ton a day!

Yes, Apatosaurus
Was enormous,
And did little else but eat.
A giant who,
I think it's true,
You *might* have liked to meet.

SMALL DINOSAUR

Many a Dinosaur was large,
But a few were swift and small.
Ornitholestes was the name
Of one that I recall.

He raced about the reptile world,
Eating creatures even smaller,
While escaping the clutch of monsters
Who were heavier and taller.

He raced about for ever so long,
As slim as a salamander.
And who can say he'd have done so well,
If he'd been a whole lot grander?

DENTISTS AND DINOSAURS

The Dinosaurs
    Had lots of teeth,
Some up above,
    Some underneath,
And yet they got
    No dental care,
Because there were
    No dentists there.

No dentists there
    To give relief,
When reptile fangs
    Had come to grief,
No dental care,
    Their pain to slake,
When giant gums
    Would throb and ache.

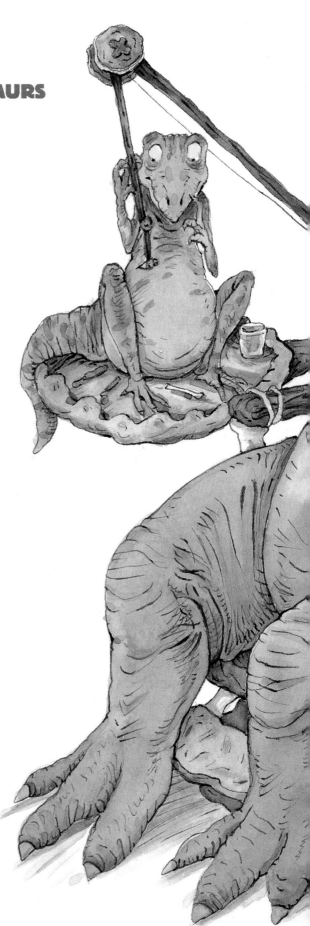

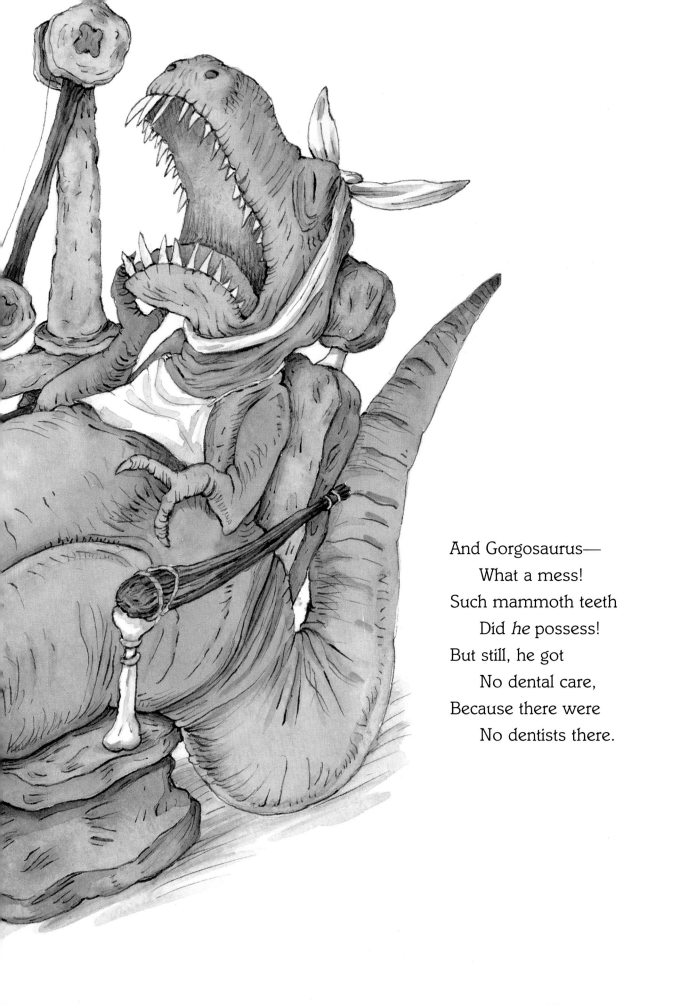

And Gorgosaurus—
    What a mess!
Such mammoth teeth
    Did *he* possess!
But still, he got
    No dental care,
Because there were
    No dentists there.

SHY DINOSAUR

I think that it's truly a shame
How *some* reptiles have so little fame.
Camptosaurus, shown here,
Is forgotten, I fear,
And I don't know who's really to blame.

"Camptosaurus?" I now hear you say.
"Did he chase, did he pounce, did he slay?
He was timid and small,
And ate no one at all?
Then why *should* he be famous today?"

Well, that creature knew how to survive,
And though shy, he continued to thrive.
Others died off completely,
But he lived on discreetly,
And should be famed just for staying alive.

THE BIG CLAW

If you and I, in ancient days,
    Had met grim Deinonychus,
We would have seen his awful claws,
    And *hoped* that he might like us!

Those claws of his could open you
    As swiftly as a zipper,
And that's why some have called the beast
    An early Jack the Ripper!

THE DINO BALL

I saw last night
The strangest sight,
Twelve Dinos at a ball.
Some wore silk shirts,
Some velvet skirts,
And some, no clothes at all.

One said, "My dear,
It's good you're here,
Our scene is quite insane!
It's dance and sing,
And have a fling,
When reptiles entertain!"

One said, "Let's bake
A chocolate cake,
And then we'll all have tea!"
One said, "It's best
To eat the guest!"
And then she glared at *me*.

"But I'm not nutritious,
Or delicious!"
I cried in fear and dread.
Then came a roar
From that Dinosaur,
And I woke up—safe in bed!

ALLOSAURUS MAKES HER APOLOGY

"**O**h, listen!" Allosaurus said,
    "And sympathize with me!
My tummy feels so empty,
    I'm as hungry as can be!

"I'm called bad names!" the reptile sobbed.
    "I'm never understood!
But when you're huge and famished,
    It's not easy to be good!

"Oh, listen!" cried the Dinosaur,
    "Though monster I appear,
I cannot help my appetite—
    And now I'll eat you, dear!"

TALE OF A TAIL

Ankylosaurus walked around,
    Waved her tail above the ground.
Awkward creature, clumsy, slow,
    Never could outrun her foe.

Wore thick armor, head to feet,
    Protecting her from those she'd meet.
And then, besides her "coat of mail,"
    That reptile owned a vicious tail.

A rocklike club she had to show
  Some savage and carnivorous foe,
Which often made the foe turn 'round,
  To find another battleground.

Yet if and when she *had* to fight,
  That tough old soldier did all right,
For when her armor proved too frail,
  Ankylosaurus swung her tail!

THE AWFUL THREE

Some Dinosaurs were homely,
    As homely as could be,
But most were really beautiful
    Compared with "The Awful Three."

"The Awful Three" I call them,
    A family to curl your hair,
The flying Pterodactyls,
    Three monsters of the air.

The first was Rhamphorhynchus,
    Hardly longer than your arm,
A grisly little monster
    With very little charm.

In time small Rhamphorhynchus
    Was succeeded by another,
The heftier Dimorphodon,
    His Pterodactyl brother.

Dimorphodon ate fishes,
    And numerous insects too,
And he, in turn, was followed
    By the last of that ghastly crew.

The last of the Pterodactyls
    Was giant Pteranodon,
By far the spookiest monster
    I ever gazed upon.

But Pteranodon is gone now,
    Gone from the empty air,
And *I* for one am happy
    That *she's* no longer there.

DINOSAUR NOISES

*T*hump! Thump! Thump!
   The Dinosaurs are walking.
Grunt! Grunt! Grunt!
   The Dinosaurs are talking.

Munch! Munch! Munch!
   The Dinosaurs are eating.
Burp! Burp! Burp!
   It's their stomachs overheating.

DINOSAUR BABIES

Some Dinosaur babies
    Had a life that was sad,
For they never knew Mom,
    And they never knew Dad.

Some Dinosaur mothers
    Seemed sort of hard-hearted,
They left their eggs *somewhere*,
    And then they departed!

But *one* mother there was
    Who cared for her brood.
Maiasaura made sure
    That her babies had food.

She loved all her children,
    And not one was a waif,
As she guarded them all,
    And kept them all safe.

IF A DINOSAUR CAME TO YOUR SCHOOL

If a Dinosaur came to your school,
    And said, "I'm the Substitute Teacher!"
Would you stand there and gape like a fool,
    Or flee the reptilian creature?

If a Dinosaur came to your house,
    And said, "I believe you're my niece!"
Would you run off and hide like a mouse,
    Or calmly call up the police?

If a Dinosaur climbed in your bath,
    And cried, "Water is best when it's steaming!"
Would you hurl a wet towel in wrath,
    Or cross fingers—and hope you were dreaming!

THE GHOST OF STEGOSAURUS

It's said the ghost of Stegosaurus
    Met a scholar once,
Who sneered, "Your brain was very small!
    I'm sure you were a dunce!"

Well, Stegosaurus thought a bit,
    Then said, "I guess you're right.
I've heard that Man is very smart,
    While Dinos weren't too bright.

"And yet, for fifty million years
    We Steggies roamed the Earth,
A rather decent life-span
    For a beast of little worth!

"So, while it's true that Man is bright—
    On this we both agree—
Can we be sure, with all his brains,
    He'll last as long as *me*?"

THE DANGEROUS ANCIENT SEAS

Within the dangerous ancient seas
    Some giant reptiles grew.
An awesome sight, by day or night,
    Each time they swam in view.

In one bold, hungry family
    Were the many Ichthyosaurs.
All swift and strong, some six yards long,
    They ruled the ocean floors.

Next came the portly Plesiosaurs,
    And lots of food *they* needed.
To eat more fish was their great wish,
    And most times they succeeded.

Another family showed up too,
    The menacing Mosasaurs,
As fierce and ferocious, as cruel and atrocious,
    As any great Dinosaurs.

Yes, giant reptiles splashed about,
    Cavorting at their ease,
And hopes were dim, if you took a swim,
    In those dangerous ancient seas.

THE TYRANT KING

Listen to him roar and growl!
　　The Tyrant King is on the prowl!

Run for cover! Save your necks!
　　It's Tyrannosaurus Rex!

Best forget your foolish pride.
　　Now's the time to go and hide.

Sink beneath the swampy water,
　　And you might escape the slaughter.

Friends, I needn't tell you twice,
　　If T. Rex gets you, it's not nice!

Oh, listen to him growl and roar!
　　The Tyrant King has come once more!

A RUFF GUY

Oh, what a curious sight is here,
   Triceratops, I mean.
One more great monster to appear
   Upon the reptile scene.

Around his neck, a monstrous ruff,
   Four legs of monstrous size,
And if these features weren't enough,
   Those horns above his eyes!

Sometimes his enemy would fight,
   And sometimes turn away,
For even Tyrannosaurus might
   Not care for such a fray.

Triceratops, Triceratops,
   His horns were long and keen,
One more great monster to appear
   Upon the reptile scene.

DINOSAURS FOREVER!

Most experts say the Dinosaurs
    Have been dead for countless Ages,
The fierce, the sly, the bold, the shy,
    That march across these pages.

But as long as there are those of us
Who love "The Beast that Roars,"
No matter what the experts say—
There will *always* be Dinosaurs!